James Duggan

# Reminiscences and Impressions of a Visit to Rome During the Canonization of the Japanese Martyrs

A Lecture Pronounced in Bryan Hall, Dec. 18th, 1862

James Duggan

**Reminiscences and Impressions of a Visit to Rome During the Canonization of the Japanese Martyrs**
*A Lecture Pronounced in Bryan Hall, Dec. 18th, 1862*

ISBN/EAN: 9783337168681

Printed in Europe, USA, Canada, Australia, Japan

Cover: Foto ©Andreas Hilbeck / pixelio.de

More available books at **www.hansebooks.com**

# REMINISCENCES AND IMPRESSIONS

OF

# A VISIT TO ROME,

DURING THE

## Canonization of the Japanese Martyrs,

A LECTURE,

PRONOUNCED IN BRYAN HALL, DEC. 18TH, 1862,

BY

RIGHT REV. JAMES DUGGAN,
BISHOP OF CHICAGO.

CHICAGO:
PUBLISHED BY J. J. KEARNEY, 167 SOUTH CLARK STREET.

1863.

CHICAGO, Dec. 9th, 1862.

RT. REV. JAMES DUGGAN:

*Dear Sir:*—We would respectfully request that you will repeat the lecture lately delivered by you, on the subject of your recent visit to Rome, and of the ceremonies attending the Canonization of the Japanese Martyrs. We feel that in this request we express the desire of a large portion of the public who were unable to hear it; and that a proper and charitable result may commend this request to your favorable consideration, we will arrange for the use of Bryan Hall on such evening as may suit your convenience, and appropriate to the benefit of the poor the proceeds that may be realized from this most interesting and instructive lecture.

Yours most respectfully,

| | |
|---|---|
| J. YOUNG SCAMMON, | R. T. MERRICK, |
| GEO. P. A. HEALY, | S. S. HAYES, |
| JAS. W. SHEEHAN, | W. F. STOREY, |
| C. C. PARKS, | J. DEVELIN, |
| F. C. SHERMAN, | A. B. CHAPOTON, |
| B. E. MORRIS, | B. M. THOMAS, |
| JAS. ROBB, | M. TIERNAN, |
| THOS. HOYNE, | B. G. CAULFIELD, |
| M. D. GILMAN, | D. BRAINARD, |
| THOS. B. BRYAN, | WM. BROSS, |
| | JNO. L. WILSON. |

---

CHICAGO, Dec. 11th, 1862.

GENTLEMEN:

Though unaccustomed to repeat what I have once delivered, and though reluctant to appear in a public capacity, I still feel that in the present instance I should not decline an invitation having so charitable an object in view.

I shall, therefore, hold myself prepared to comply with your request on any evening during the next week which you shall judge most convenient.

I remain, gentlemen,

Faithfully Yours in Christ

† JAMES DUGGAN,

Bishop of Chicago.

Messrs. J. YOUNG SCAMMON, M. D. GILMAN, R. T. MERRICK, G. P. A. HEALY, F. C. SHERMAN, and others.

CHICAGO, DEC. 20th, 1862.

*Rt. Rev'd and Dear Sir:*—The undersigned, Committee, respectfully request, on behalf of the gentlemen at whose solicitation you delivered a Lecture at Bryan Hall, on the 18th inst., that you would furnish them with a copy for publication in pamphlet form, that they may gratify the general desire to possess so interesting and instructive a paper.

With great respect,

Yours truly,

R. T. MERRICK,<br>
M. D. GILMAN,<br>
S. S. HAYES,<br>
J. DEVELIN,<br>
B. G. CAULFIELD, } *Committee.*

RT. REV'D JAMES DUGGAN,
Bishop of Chicago.

---

CHICAGO, DEC. 21st, 1862.

*Gentlemen:*—It is not without much diffidence that I comply with your request.

In its original shape the Lecture was intended only for the sacred precincts of a Church, but it was afterwards recast and enlarged, to meet the requirements of a different place and auditory.

In its present form then, I venture, agreeably to your wishes, to address a still larger audience through the medium of the press.

I remain, gentlemen,

Truly yours in Christ,

† JAMES DUGGAN,

Bishop of Chicago.

Messrs. M. D. GILMAN, R. T. MERRICK, S. S. HAYES, B. G. CAULFIELD, I. DEVELIN.

# LECTURE.

---

I HAVE been asked by some prominent gentlemen of this city to deliver a discourse for the relief of the poor among us, especially for the benefit of the widows and orphans, now, alas! in these disastrous days, likely to be more numerous than ever, and have not felt myself at liberty to decline; at the same time it was suggested that reminiscences and impressions of my late visit to Rome, and particularly of the great solemnity in which I was so happy as to participate, would prove to be an acceptable topic to many. In the justice of this suggestion I could not but concur, for the grand ceremony in St. Peter's, on that memorable 8th of June, has not only a deep spiritual significance and powerful attraction in itself, but, viewed as an ecclesiastical function, casts into the shade all the most gorgeous pageants of modern times.

The very name, too, of Rome, has a magical influence, and bears with it an interest that can never wane; for what city can for a moment compare in attraction with the venerable capital, coeval with so many centuries, whose pavement has been trodden by so many generations, and from whose bosom have gone forth those sacred, mysterious influences which for so many centuries have swayed the minds and hearts of the civilized, yes, and even of the uncivilized world?

The subject, then, of this discourse, bears with it its own interest. I propose to present to you a rapid sketch of my journey to the Holy City, some incidents of the way, my impressions during my sojourn in Rome, the imposing scene of the canonization, in the grandest temple which the art of man has raised for the purposes of religion, or for any other purpose whatever; concluding with a view of the present position of the Holy Father in relation to "the patrimony of St. Peter," and to his own subjects—a topic of vital importance to many at the present time, and of lively interest to all.

During the past winter, letters were issued by the Cardinal Prefect to the Bishops of the Catholic world, inviting them to Rome for the solemnity of the Canonization of the Japanese Martyrs, to take place in St. Peter's, on the 8th of June. It was stated, at the same time, that a visit to Rome, on that occasion, would be particularly grateful to the Holy Father, tried as he was by various afflictions. No command was implied, merely a simple invitation was given, and that not emanating directly from the Holy Father himself, yet the result was an assemblage of Bishops, from all parts of the world, such as history has never before recorded.

In compliance with this invitation, in the company of five other American Prelates, I sailed in the Canada for Europe on the 30th of April in the present year.

The voyage, the incidents of which I cannot pause to recount, was exceedingly agreeable, owing to the charm of the company on board, amongst whom were our late Minister to the Court of Rome, and other intelligent gentlemen from various parts of the country.

I pass over the strange scenes and impressions that strike the eye of the traveler long unaccustomed to Europe—the varied beauty of Ireland—the richness and grandeur of England—the magnificence, the splendor, and the gaiety of France,—until we find ourselves in Marseilles. At that port, my friend and companion,—a neighboring prelate,—and myself, were to embark for the Roman harbor of Civita Vecchia. On the evening of May 26th, at the hour of ten o'clock, we stood on board the "Posilipo," bound for that port. The night was dark and the vessel crowded to excess—the Company monopolizing that service having, it would seem, made no provision for the unusual throng of travelers. We soon found ourselves among friends. Well known voices from home and other regions soon greeted us, and in such a joyous meeting all inconvenience was soon forgotten.

As our steamer moved from the port we were startled for a moment by unexpected and repeated cheers, that went up from dense throngs surrounding us, as we fancied, on every side. They came from the friends of the bishops, and of many others on board, and prolonged cries of "Vive le Pape," "Vive Pie IX," were mingled with the most enthusiastic cheers for their own immediate friends.

The following morning revealed to us the number and quality of our "*compagnons de voyage.*" We had on board nine Archbishops, including two Cardinals, and twenty-five Bishops, representing various regions of the globe. There were also large numbers of ecclesiastics of every grade, of Religions of either sex, and very many of the laity, making the pilgrimage to Rome. That happy day on the blue Mediterranean was spent in most delightful converse. Never was there a more cordial and fraternal union than amongst those who, for the greater part, met as strangers, but were soon friends and brothers. As it was the month of Mary, our devotions to the "Star of the Sea" were not forgotten. An altar, crowned by a statue of the Virgin, arose in the centre of the vessel as if by magic, and seldom were the praises of the "Immaculate One" chanted with more fervent piety, or with greater solemnity. The leader of our choir, Hermann, is one famous for his musical abilities, as well as for his personal history. He was a Jew, but is now, not only a convert to the Catholic faith, but wears the habit and cord of St. Francis. Never before had he associated with him so venerable a choir. Around him stood Cardinals, Archbishops, Bishops, some French officers, Religious in the habits of their respective Orders, with large numbers of the laity from many lands. Solemn and tender was the devotion of that assembly, and as the shades of the calm evening gathered around us, the last tones of the "Ave Maris Stella," "Hail Star of the Sea," died along the azure waters of the "Midland Sea." The scene, too, was in harmony with the occasion. To the right were the islands of Ajaccio and Elba—historic names—and on our left the undulating shores of beauteous Italy: above us the soft sky of that genial clime, reflected in the now roseate waters of the "tideless sea." The affecting Vesper Service was closed by an eloquent and touching address delivered with great animation by the learned Bishop of Tulle.

Early on the following morning we found ourselves in the harbor of Civita Vecchia. A salute from the fortress announced our arrival, and welcomed us as honored guests to the "Patrimony of St. Peter." On landing, a dignitary conducted us to the Legate, who received us with warm and dignified courtesy, and invited all the Cardinals and Bishops to a bountiful repast. In this we had a foretaste of the welcome awaiting us in the Eternal City. Refreshed by a refined and generous hospitality, we took places about noon in the train for Rome. This rapid mode of conveyance might at first seem strangely out of place in Italy, and destructive of the charm of travel in that romantic land; but to the traveler who had already journeyed that forty miles in dusty and fatiguing "*vettura*," it was indeed pleasant to find himself now whirled along over the same distance by steam. We passed along the shore of the Sapphire sea, with the bleak Campagna before us, so appropriately the foreground and introductive to the once proud metropolis of the world, and even still the most affecting and interesting city in the universe. Though shorn to a great extent of her earthly splendor, she may yet be appropriately addressed in the words of St. Prosper, who had himself gazed on the dying glories of the mistress of the ancient world:

> "Sedes Roma Petri, quæ pastoralis honoris,
> Facta Caput mundo, quidquid non possidet armis
> Religione tenet."
> "Rome, Peter's See, the world doth still obey;
> The empire won by arms, is held by Faith's bless'd sway."

Though only the 28th of May, the fields were already white with the harvest in that genial clime and fertile soil. The laborers come from a distance to work, during the day, on that rich but unhealthy plain; their bright colors and high-peaked hats, their dark lustrous eyes and sun-burnt complexions, the dun-colored buffaloes, the blue sky and ripening grain, many an ancient tower and venerable ruin reflected in the blue waters, combined to present to us, some of the well-known features of Italian landscape.

The noble pile of St. Paul's Basilica, rising phœnix-like from its ashes, more magnificent than ever, reminded us that we were approaching the "eternal walls" of Rome. After an absence of more than ten years I could not behold them again without emotion; for when has the cultivated traveler ever turned his back on the ancient city without regret, or does not again hail it with delight? For where else can he find assembled all that is holiest to enlighten the mind,—all that is most touching to affect the heart? On what other spot of earth can he find concentrated the interest of the world for nearly three thousand years? Where else can he discover whatever is noblest and most perfect in Art to charm the imagination, and to improve the taste? Rome, though shorn of her earthly glories, is still the mistress of the world; still she maintains her universal "empire over mind, undiminished;" she is still the favorite home of religion, of science, of refinement;

> "Still
> The fount, at which the panting mind assuages
> Her thirst of knowledge, quaffing there her fill,
> Flows from the eternal source of Rome's imperial hill."

The words addressed to her by a brilliant, but unhappy genius, too noted for his hostility to her teaching, and to Christianity in every form, would seem appropriate to her throughout all time:

> "Rome, dont le destin, dans la paix, dans la guerre,
> Est d'etre en tous les temps, maitresse de la terre."

> "Rome, heaven awards the world for thy domain;
> As once in war, in peace is now thy reign."

In the hospitable walls of the American College, surrounded by dear friends, we soon found ourselves at home, and in the greetings and intercourse of such minds, all the unpleasant incidents and fatigues of our long journey were soon atoned for, and recalled no more.

On the following morning, May 29th, all the Cardinals and Bishops in Rome, were assembled in the Basilica of St. John Lateran, to celebrate the Feast of the Ascension, and to meet the Holy Father, who was to be present on the occasion. This magnificent church is the Cathedral of Rome, and is first in dignity of all the churches in the world. This priority of dignity is announced by an inscription on its front: "*Omnium Ecclesiarum Urbis et Orbis, Mater et Caput,*"—the Mother and Head of all the Churches of the City, and of the World. It was founded by the first Christian Emperor Constantine, and its majesty and riches are worthy of its antiquity and of its dignity. As we enter its grand portal what a striking spectacle greets the eye! At our left is the Corsini Chapel, which, in rare marbles, in monuments, and in the style of its architecture, is perhaps the richest and most beautiful in the world. One beholds with delight the golden vault over head, the precious and graceful pillars of *verd antique*, and the colossal statues of the twelve Apostles that meet our gaze as we pass. Before us is the gothic canopy over the grand altar—a monument of the arts in bygone days. We take our seats in view of the Chapel of the Holy Sacrament, the tabernacle of which gleams with the costliest gems, and having its canopy sustained by the celebrated fluted pillars of bronze taken from the temple of Jupiter Capitolinus —miracles of art and beauty. Mouldering from the enamelled roof, hangs an ancient, time-worn standard, emblazoned with the symbol of the Saracen—a trophy of the victory by which the glory of the Crescent went down forever before the the Cross in the gulf of Lepanto.

In the semi-circular tribune behind the altar, the Cardinals clad in purple costume have taken their places, the Archbishops and Bishops are placed on the right, and an immense concourse of people from many lands fill the magnificent hall of the ancient temple. There is a slight commotion in the Church; the eyes of all are for a moment directed towards the altar, and the well known form of Pius IX, clad in white, appears, followed by a detachment of the noble guard, and various members of his household. More than ten years had elapse,d since I last looked on that venerable and benignant countenance, which instantly wins all who behold it. Considering the trials through which he passed of late, I had expected to find many proofs of suffering in his frame. But no! His face was as mild, and as benignant as ever. The flight of ten years had scarcely left a trace behind. His step was light and elastic, and his voice raised in benediction and prayer resounded through the "Mother and Parent of Churches" in tones as full, and as musical as ever.

The solemn High Mass, celebrated by one of the Cardinals, being concluded, he was accompanied by Cardinals and prelates to the balcony of the Church to bestow the Apostolic Benediction on the city, and on the world, "*Urbi et Orbi.*" That impressive spectacle no one who witnessed it can ever forget. The place in which we stood, the view of the city before us, the immense multitude filling the piazza of St. John's, the Pontifical and French troops drawn up in the distance,—all formed a varied—a most striking picture. On one side were the ruins of ancient aqueducts, and of other monuments of the past, covering the desolate Campagna—the Sabine Hills—the Alban Mount once crowned by the Temple of Jupiter Latiaris reflected in the lakes of Albano and Nemi,—on the other, the mighty Coliseum, the Palatine Mount, the distant Tiber—the stairs from Pilate's hall, once trodden by Divine feet,—before us the highest obelisk known, the venerable walls of Rome, the Basilica of Santa Croce, and "numbers whom no man could number" waiting in reverent attitudes for the blessing of the Father of the Faithful. In full and harmonious tones was that blessing sung, and as the last notes of the words of benediction died away, the tidings were proclaimed to the city from the cannon's mouth, and the acclamations of the multitude rent the air. Never before did I witness such a scene of pious enthusiasm. The troops presented arms, whilst loud and prolonged cheers of "Evviva

Pio IX." "Vive le Pape," "Viva Pio Nono, Pontefice Re," were long re-echoed by the Church and Palace of the Lateran.

This was the first demonstration which I witnessed of the warm attachment of the Romans to their gentle and paternal Ruler. Many others and still more enthusiastic, I afterwards beheld. An idea, I know, prevails, one most industriously circulated, that the Pope is disliked by his own subjects. I most cordially assert that all I saw, and could otherwise learn on that subject during my residence in Rome, tended to impress me with the very opposite conviction. Never was temporal ruler followed with such acclamations as was Pio Nono during my sojourn in his city. He was every where hailed as the Sovereign of hearts, and affections.

Doubtless, the revolutionary party has spared no effort to excite disaffection in Rome, and to some extent it may have succeeded. But under what form of government, I ask, are all content? Is the disaffection of a few, or even of many, a proof of the incapacity of a Sovereign, or of the inefficiency of a government? If such be the test of failure or success, then every government has failed in its duties, and all government is impossible.

During a special audience given to the American Bishops, the Holy Father spoke freely of the condition of his temporal affairs. The interview was most interesting and affecting. We were received with all the kindness and gentleness so characteristic of Pio Nono. After some congratulations had passed, and various topics were discussed, he came to his temporal difficulties. "We were aware," he said, "of the straits to which he was reduced by the enemies of the Holy See, and the despoilers of the property of the Church. Various terms and compromises had been offered him, the end of which was to leave them in possession of their sacrilegious spoils, and to ratify their iniquity. To all of which he had but one answer to give—'restore the property of the Church;' to alienate, or dispose of that was not in his power. His unvarying reply was '*non possumus*,' the answer given by the Apostles to the tyrants of old. The same reply he would continue to make, undismayed by the frowns, unmoved by the blandishments of power. As to himself, he would yield only to brute force. He would quit the city only when compelled,"—an assertion he accompanied by a gesture intimating his resolve to remain in Rome unless forced to yield. All this was said with a mildness not to be ruffled, but with a firmness not to be shaken. Some more conversation on other topics terminated this memorable interview.

Before leaving the Vatican we called, as was customary, on Cardinal Antonelli, the Secretary of State. I need not add that we were greeted with that high-bred courtesy, and warmth for which he is well known. The same views were here repeated in regard to the Holy Father and the States of the Church. I must add too, that he showed deep sympathy for this country, in the calamity that had befallen it, and frequently gave expression to his regret for the troubles of so great a Nation. Indeed the same sympathy and regret were every where to be found among the officials of the Roman government.

In such a city as Rome, and with the society which it then particularly afforded, it may be presumed that the days intervening between our arrival, and the Solemnity of the Canonization, were constantly, and most agreeably employed. If Cicero could say in his own day, that he was treading on the footprints of history when he walked her streets, how must those monuments have accumulated, and the interest attached to them increased, after the flight and vicissitudes of more than two thousand years! Rome, ancient and modern—pagan and Christian,—classic and religious,—lies before us. Wherever we tread, 'tis holy ground. The sacred dust of saints and martyrs hallows its soil. On every side the relics of the saints and servants of God inspire devotion, and fill the soul with holy awe. We bent in reverence over their sacred remains contained in ancient sarcophagi, or costly shrine. The sites and even the walls of the houses in which they once dwelt are pointed out, the places of their martyrdom and sanctification well known. The magnificent shrines in which their precious relics repose, the glorious temples raised over their ashes, tell us of the piety of past ages. Every where we meet the most touching memorials of the good, and great, of every age, and almost of every clime.

Inclosed within the walls of the City, or situated immediately around them, we can number more than three hundred and sixty churches, besides innumerable other monuments of Christian piety and benevolence. There are few of those that do not claim a special regard for their history, their architecture, and the master-pieces of painting, and sculpture adorning their precincts. The new Church of St. Paul's on the 'Ostian way,' almost rivals the hitherto unapproachable glories of St. Peter's. Its charming collonades, the precious marbles encrusting its walls, the mosaic pavement beneath our feet, the mosaic portraits of all the Popes on its entablature, the unique pillars of alabaster, presented by the Viceroy of Egypt, now supporting the canopy over the high altar, the view of its arcades and aisles, and fretted roof burnished with gold—all tell us of the deep religious spirit which planned, and accomplished, so majestic a monument of Religion in our own days.

The scholar, too, hails with rapture, places and names familiar to him almost from infancy. He beholds with feelings of mournful admiration all that remains of ancient Rome. He ascends the Capitol, and finds the graceful columns of the temple of Jupiter Capitolinus adorning the Church of 'Ara Coeli,' erected on its site. He wanders through the Forum, and beholds only a triumphal arch, and a few erect columns that have withstood the shock of time. He walks on the ancient pavement of the 'Via Sacra,' and recalls in prose and verse, the well sung glories of other days. That heap of "ruin upon ruins" to his right is the Palatine Mount, and all he shall discover of the Palace of the Cæsars. He passes various, nameless temples and ruins, walks beneath the arch of Titus, and looks with awe on the mighty Coliseum.

> "And here the buzz of eager Nations ran,
> In murmured pity, or loud roared applause,
> As man was slaughtered by his fellow man."

A few short excursions show him all that time and war have spared of the great City that once ruled the world. Not only does he trace the seven hills, but spread out before him are the colossal ruins of the most dazzling earthly grandeur. From those he can form an idea of the greatness of the people who raised them, as from the broken columns and fallen capitals at his feet, he can re-construct the monuments they once supported and adorned. He can enter too, into the feelings of the ancient Roman who hailed his city, as the most lovely of all things, "*rerum pulcherrima Roma*,"—as the chosen seat of the Divinity—the light of civilization to the world—as the glorious mistress of the Universe!

With such scenes and monuments to contemplate, surely time could not lie heavily on our hands. The Cardinals too, and various other dignitaries, invited the strangers to their residences. In those noble homes, adorned by the works of genius, were assembled in familiar intercourse—illustrious persons—venerable forms bowed by the weight of years, and dignities—men famous for their virtues and talents—celebrated writers and artists from many lands—all were here blended in a familiar interchange of sentiments and ideas. In such occupations, and in the enjoyment of the society of the illustrious and the good, from all parts of the earth, the day fixed for the grand solemnity rapidly approached.

On the morning of the Feast of Pentecost, the 8th of June, the Cardinals and Bishops met at the early hour of 7 o'clock, for the long expected ceremony. The place appointed for this meeting was the Sistine Chapel in the Vatican. Its walls are animated by "many a prophet and many a saint,"—models of perfect art. Over our heads still live the grand conceptions of Michael Angelo, among which shines conspicuous the "Temptation of our first Parents," one of his most beautiful creations. Before us over the altar, appears in awful distinctness the "Final Judgment,"—the most terrific monument of his stern genius.

After a brief delay the grand procession was formed for St. Peter's. The Cardinals appeared in golden vestments and silken mitres, the Bishops in copes and linen mitres, and the rest of the clergy, secular and regular, in habiliments suitable to their rank and order.

Onward, at length, moved the gorgeous assemblage, an immense body of clergy preceding the Bishops, each of whom carried waxen tapers, and chanted appropiate hymns. Down swept the illustrious *cortege*, filling the Scala Regia—the grand staircase of the Vatican—and making it vocal with songs of prayer and of praise. Perhaps no part of the solemnity that followed surpassed in striking grandeur this unequalled procession, slowly descending the marble stairs, adorned by Ionic columns, now strewn with flowers and evergreens, and lined by a serried mass of spectators. Closing this long line of clergy, Bishops and Cardinals, appears the venerable form of Pius IX, borne aloft in his chair of state, with his hand ever raised in benediction. Following him are seen the Senators and Guardians of the city, and the representatives of various Catholic lands. Slowly it glides through the grand piazza, in front of the majestic Basilica, passing the ancient Obelisk—the cotemporary of so many generations, which once, in Nero's gardens, and near its present site, looked down on the massacre of the Christians, but which, for centuries since, has recorded the triumph of the Cross.

Passing through the grand collonade, we at length enter the unrivalled Temple. Never before was its vast extent so nigh being filled as on the present occasion. The light of day was excluded for the ceremony, but thousands of waxen tapers gleam from its entablature and marble pillars, filling the sacred building with a solemn effulgence, and casting an additional splendor on its golden roof. Above the candelabra appear the portraits of the martyrs now to be canonized, with pictures descriptive of their sufferings and of their constancy. As we advance along the rich mosaic pavement the statue of many a saint seems to look down on us, as if demanding a passing reverence. The Chapel of the Blessed Sacrament being reached, the Pontiff descends to adore the Holy One, and again, at the Confessional of St. Peter, he pauses for a few moments of prayer. With reverence we pass the great Altar raised over the tomb of the first Apostles, with its canopy surmounted by the globe and cross, piercing the "wondrous dome," and sustained by four twisted pillars of bronze,—the noblest work of its kind ever known.

The Pontiff has reached his throne at the head of the Sanctuary, while the Cardinals and Bishops have taken their places on either side. On the right, and immediately behind us, appear the exiled royal family of Naples; on the left, conspicuous for their decorations, are the ambassadors of various nations to the Court of Rome. Fifty thousand spectators find ample room within the spacious walls of St. Peter's —the truly Catholic church of the world. In the midst of this imposing array, after the Cardinals and Bishops have given the usual salutation to the Pontiff, the grand solemnity begins.

We must here interrupt our narrative for a while, to explain the origin and nature of this religious display. What, then, is meant in the Catholic Church by canonization? The canonization of a saint is simply a decree by which the Sovereign Pontiff declares that a certain person has practised, during life, all Christian virtues in a heroic degree, which God Himself has attested by miracles during the life of the Saint, or by his intercession after his death. He is, in consequence, to be venerated as a saint, the Sacrifice of the Mass is to be offered to God in his honor; his name is invoked in the Litany of the Church; and his relics to be exposed to the reverence of the Faithful.

In the early ages of the Church the rite of canonization consisted in the mere insertion of the name of a martyr in the Canon of the Mass. The piety of the first Christians raised an altar over his relics, on which the Sacrifice of the Mass was offered. Around those "Martyria" they assembled on the anniversary of the martyr's triumph, especially when the acts recording the martyrdom were publicly read.

Some centuries later, we find the Bishops reserving this right to themselves, as it was for them to judge who had really laid down his life as a witness to the Christian Faith. Accordingly, the names judged worthy of that honor were enrolled in the Martyrologies and Dyptichs of the various churches. When peace was restored to the Church, we find the same high distinction conferred on those who, though, they had no opportunity of shedding their blood for their faith, were still its faithful witnesses before God, by the holiness of their lives, their victory over themselves and the world, their apostolic labors, and for eminent services rendered to man through love of their Divine Master.

Towards the close of the tenth century, it was deemed advisable to reserve the act of canonization to the judgment of the Holy See alone. The first instance we have of this solemn ceremony being performed by the Sovereign Pontiff, is the canonization of Ulric, Bishop of Augsburg, (whose sacred relics I had the happiness recently to venerate,) by John XV., in the year 993. The second example we read of, is that of St. Simeon, of Treves, by Benedict VIII, in 1042. Innocent III, by a Bull dated April 3, 1200, confirmed forever the Constitution of Alexander III, who reserved this rite to the wisdom and discretion of Rome exclusively.

Previous to the solemn act a most severe scrutiny is made into the life and character of the individual presented for this high dignity. His entire career from the cradle to the grave, his actions, his conversation, his writings, are all examined and weighed with the most rigid impartiality. Commissions of cardinals and other high dignitaries are appointed to sift the evidences and testimonies offered, and every possible precaution is taken to arrive at the exact truth. Public prayers are ordered in the churches of Rome, the light of the Holy Spirit, always promised to the Church, is fervently implored, and the Divine aid unceasingly invoked. After this rigid scrutiny and fervent prayer, the person presented is merely Beatified, which is not a solemn declaration of sanctity, but a simple permission for a religious community, or a certain diocese or nation, to venerate a servant of God. A long period must still elapse before the Beatified can be Canonized. During that interval the same rigid examination continues, and above all, the miracles ascribed to the saint or martyr are submitted to the severest tests. So impartial and minute is this protracted scrutiny that all deception is impossible.

A Roman prelate presented a report of one of these commissions to an English gentleman, not a member of the Catholic Church, who, after its perusal, exclaimed: "If all the miracles recognized by the Church of Rome were as clearly proved as those, I should have no hesitation in subscribing to them." "And yet," replies the Prelate, "of all those miracles which appear to you so clearly proved, the Congregation of Rites has *not admitted even one*, because the evidence did not seem sufficiently strong."

And who were they who were now to receive this high honor of being solemnly enrolled amongst the saints and friends of God before the entire Christian world? Were they of that class which the world delights to honor? Were they illustrious by their birth, powerful connexions, or their riches? Ah no! Of that number three were priests of the humble order of St. Francis. Their badge was the cowl and the cord; their only arms, the Cross. To these were added some lay brothers of the same Order, some more of the Society of Jesus, and the rest were of the laity, but of the third Order of St. Francis. Of this band of Christian heroes all but six were natives of Japan. But of this band of heroes some had, like the Apostles, left friends and home, and all that man holds most dear on earth, to extend the domain of Christ, to enlighten barbarous lands, and they still further imitated their illustrious models by laying down their lives for their Master. Thus did they fulfill in themselves the divine test of perfect faith and love. "Greater love than this no man hath when he lays down his life for his friends." They were amongst the first victims of the persecution commenced against the Christians in Japan in 1596. The holiness of their lives condemned the licentiousness of the court of Taico-Sama. The old cry so familiar to paganism, "*Christianos ad leones*," was now raised against them. They excited, forsooth, disaffection in the Empire. To the number of twenty-six those soldiers of the Cross were arrested and condemned to death. Of this band three were mere boys, in their twelfth, thirteenth and fifteenth years. On the 3rd of February, 1597, those holy victims were led to execution on the "Mount of Martyrs," one of the hills of Nagasaki, where crosses had already been raised. With joy they embraced them like the Apostle St. Andrew. With their garments were they bound to those altars of suffering, and whilst their eyes were raised to heaven, their suspended forms were transfixed with a lance. They rejoiced in their torments, and like the first Martyr, prayed for their executioners.

Urban VIII pronounced them martyrs, and beatified them in 1627. Such, in brief, is their history; forgotten, indeed, by the world, but written in the book of the undying remembrance of God's Church. That Mother never forgets her children. Her love follows them to the most distant lands, and survives their earthly doom. Their barbarous murderers had doubtless forgotten the names of their victims, and, perhaps, the very circumstances of their cruel death. With what surprise must their descendants now hear of such extraordinary honor paid to men put to an ignominious death as criminals by those of their own nation. And how great must be the wonder of those Japanese Ambassadors so lately feasted among us, and of others still more recently visiting various parts of Europe during those days when the Christian world was so profoundly moved at this public veneration of those men, for the vindication of a principle which their own laws punished as a crime? Alas! It is not for them to recognize the divine heroism of Faith, its glories, its triumphs and its rewards. But from these reflections we must hasten to glance at the imposing rite itself.

All is now ready for the grand ceremony. The Pontiff, from his chair, can behold an array of Cardinals and Bishops, on either hand, such as neither he, or his predecessors witnessed before. Around the great Altar, where the bronze cornucopiæ keep perpetual watch before the Apostles' tomb, are arranged the Swiss and Noble Guards. Multitudes of reverent worshippers throng the gorgeous mosaic pavement. The great temple seems almost filled. The blaze of thousands of wax lights supplies the place of day, diffusing a "solemn, dim, religious light," so suitable to the occasion. On either hand is royalty discrowned, and many of the sovereignties of the earth, in the persons of their representatives. In the midst of this profound expectation, the Cardinal Procurator advances to the Pontifical throne. He is attended by the Consistorial Advocate, who, on his knees, prefers the following petition: "Most Holy Father, the Most Reverend Cardinal N., here present, urgently (*instanter*,) asks that those persons, N., N., N., be inscribed by your Holiness in the catalogue of the Saints of our Lord Jesus Christ, and that their venerable names may be pronounced as Saints by all faithful Christians." The Secretary of Briefs replies in the name of the Pontiff, "that the virtues and merits of those blessed souls are well known to him, but he must still invoke God, through the intercession of the Blessed Virgin, the holy Apostles SS. Peter and Paul, and of all the other Saints."

All instantly fall on their knees, and the song of prayer and supplication to the Saints resounds. It was like the sound of many waters, "sweet as from blest voices," ringing through the golden hall and hallowed aisles of the matchless temple.

The Litanies concluded, the Procurator again appears before the throne, and still more urgently (*instantius*,) prefers the same petition. A similar reply is given, and the Pontiff intones, on bended knee, the invocation to the Divine Spirit, "*Veni Sancte Spiritus*," imploring that heavenly light promised the Church for all time, but, most especially for momentous occasions like the present.

At the termination of the sublime hymn, the Cardinal Procurator stands for the third time before the Pontifical Chair, and most urgently (*instantissime*,) puts up the same supplication. The sovereign Pontiff then, seated on his throne, and with mitre on, pronounces, in the midst of solemn silence, the form of canonization:

"To the honor of the holy and undivided Trinity, for the exaltation of the Catholic Faith, and the increase of the Christian religion, by the authority of our Lord Jesus Christ, and of the Holy Apostles SS. Peter and Paul, and by our own, after mature deliberation, and after having consulted our Venerable Brothers the Cardinals of the Holy Roman Church, the Patriarchs, Archbishops and Bishops in our city, we define and decree that those blessed ones, N., N., N., N., are Saints, and we inscribe them in the catalogue of the Saints, decreeing that their memory be celebrated every year by the entire Church with devotion, on the days of their birth, in the name of the Father, and of the Son, and of the Holy Ghost. Amen."

A murmur of prayer breaks the silence of the vast multitude, oppressed by the awful scene. The Pontiff intones that song of rapturous praise, the "*Te Deum*." It is caught up by the choir and the mighty throng, who reply to each other in alternate strains. Sounds of ethereal melody from the trumpets of the Noble Guard reverberate through the building, and float aloft through the echoing dome. The great bell of the Basilica peals the glad tidings to the city. It is answered by the bell of the Capitol and innumerable others from the various churches, making Rome vocal with their gladsome chimes. The solemn decree is thundered forth in salvos of artillery from Castle St. Angelo, and long re-echoed by the waves of "yellow Tiber."

Sublime and affecting was the enthusiasm of the multitudes within at this glorious termination. Few there were not dissolved in tears, or whose sobs did not choak their utterance as the chorus of prayer and thanksgiving after filling all points of the great edifice, ascended, and was borne aloft until caught up and prolonged by the blessed martyrs themselves, and the rest of the bright host who, "gathered from every nation, and tribe, and people, and tongue," stand before the throne of the Lamb, and make heaven resound with the Eternal Halleluia.

To those majestic rites succeeds the Grand Pontifical High Mass celebrated by the Sovereign Pontiff, so often, yet so imperfectly described. Yet never, even within those walls, was that sublime spectacle more impressive. The gospel was sung in Latin by the Secretary of State, Cardinal Antonelli. It was afterwards chaunted in Greek—one of the ancient languages of the Holy Scriptures, and of the Liturgy of the Church. The Pontiff still unwearied, delivered a homily on the saints just canonized, pronounced with equal fervor and energy. At the Offertory, various gifts are presented to him, all having a mystic significance, and symbolizing the virtues and perfections of those martyrs. At the consecration the guards present arms, all fall on their knees, the mighty multitude is hushed in solemn stillness, not a breath is heard throughout the mighty expanse, and as the Victim of propitiation is raised, the same unearthly music again thrills the heart, as wondrous, as indescribable, as ethereal as if issuing from the trump of an Archangel.

But we must hasten to the close of this sublime act of Religion; for who can describe it? The imposing service of seven hours duration is over, and the Pontiff, with Cardinals and Prelates, his guard and the members of his household are returning to the Vatican. Again we pass under the lofty cupola, "the Pantheon raised in the air," which attracts our eyes upwards. On the four corners of the pillars are the four Evangelists. Above them are the choirs of the blest, and high above all the Omnipotent sits enthroned in awful grandeur. The air of the vast temple is dim and smoky, thousands of the waxen lights have died in their sockets. We go out into open day, the multitude emerges from the portals of the Basilica; the great solemnity is over.

But before retiring cast a look upon that mighty host filling the piazza. It is only now you can realize the immensity of the incomparable Fane. The countless throng of bishops, of civilians, of clergy, of soldiers—all found there convenient room. With the striking contrast of dress, their emblems of various nationalities, they present a spectacle not to be seen but there. When shall the world behold any thing similar again? When shall we witness a scene so unique, so solemn, so moving, so sublime?

On the following morning the Cardinals and Prelates were again assembled in one of the large halls of the Vatican Palace. There in Consistory the Holy Father pronounced an Allocution on the state of the Church in general, and made special reference to the temporal affairs of the Holy See. He spoke of his afflictions with feeling that affected all, and with his unvarying mildness. This was followed by an address read to him in the name of all the Bishops then in Rome, and bearing their signatures. It may not be inopportune here to state that this document was drawn up by the Bishops themselves, without any dictation whatever, and was cheerfully subscribed by every bishop present. It was the spontaneous expression of their attachment to their Head, and of their warm approval of his firmness in the most trying circumstances, now poured forth in his presence. In this, as in all their other proceedings in Rome, not a single discordant voice was raised: in this tribute of duty and affection they had but one mind and one heart. He replied in a few affecting words that went to the hearts of all present.

One other scene should not be passed over in silence. The kind heart of Pius IX would gather around him in a farewell, fraternal banquet, all those Bishops who had come from afar to aid him by their support, and cheer him by their sympathy. The place selected was worthy of the occasion. It was the grand Pontifical hall of the Vatican Library, adorned by the pencils of distinguished artists. The tables were ornamented by antique vases of elaborate workmanship, and inestimable value. But in cases around those walls, lay treasures infinitely more precious still, the living words of by-gone ages inscribed on parchment, or vellum—manuscripts containing the immortal wisdom of departed genius. We wandered for some time through this unequalled repository of learning, contemplating with wonder the treasures around us. The venerable Pontiff appeared among us to welcome his guests to his home, that nothing might be wanted to the most thorough and generous hospitality. We followed him to the banquet hall, than which a more appropriate one could not be found. He is seated in the centre; near him, are the Cardinals, and extended on all sides the long line of Bishops. In this fraternal assemblage all nations were again strikingly represented. The Oriental with flowing beard and robe was seated near a prelate from Germany or France. The purple of the Bishops contrasts with the gorgeous attire of the Cardinal, or still more remarkably with the plain, white habit of the Holy Father himself. On my left was a venerable Bishop from Spain, and on my right an aged Bishop from the South of France, whose memory, stirred by the present occasion, loved to dwell in what to me was the distant past. He told of the night, when he and four hundred priests more, and an immense throng of people waited up till day had well nigh come, for the arrival of a venerable prisoner in a border village of France. It was the Saintly Pontiff Pius VII, then led into captivity. He vividly related how, as his carriage drew nigh, the entire multitude broke through the guards, and with tears and sobs implored the benediction of that afflicted, but gentle Pontiff, whose humiliation was thus changed to triumph.

In similar conversation, and various congratulations between those who there met, not as strangers, but as friends and brothers at their Father's feast, the repast was ended by a walk with the Holy Father in the Vatican Gardens. It was in such company that I looked on the aged trees, and paced the time worn walks of those gardens, that witnessed so many memorable occurrences, and are hallowed by so many memories, to all of which a new one has now been added. There, in delightful and familiar communion with the ever gracious Pius, the remainder of the afternoon flew rapidly by. Surrounded by his guests, he there addressed to us his last familiar words. Standing on the steps of a graceful Casino, he bestowed various favors on the Prelates—commissioned them to impart his benediction to their flocks, and as the day declined, pronounced, with a grace and kindness all his own, his final words of affectionate farewell. In a few moments all are dispersed, not to assemble again on earth, but all, we trust, in heaven.

But before leaving them, let us cast one last look at that illustrious body, now retiring from the gardens of the Vatican. Many there are distinguished for extraordinary virtues and dignities, and whose names are as familiar as household words in the Republic of Letters. Most of them have come from afar, and the bent forms and snowy locks of some, tell that they have almost reached the end of life's journey. It is the last time that they, and many others, too, shall visit Rome, or ever look again on such an assembly of their Brethren. Their various complexions and costumes announce their different countries. They come from all parts of Europe and America, whilst the more distant quarters of the globe are also represented. Time will not permit us to dwell especially on all, but I cannot pass over the French Episcopate without a particular notice. In the discharge of their duty on this occasion, it is well known that they disregarded the frowns and seductions of power. To the number of fifty-five they left their Diocesses for Rome, accompanied by more than three thousand of their Priests, and large numbers of their flocks. Among those Bishops were men, not only of European, but of world-wide fame—splendid intellects, whose varied acquirements reflected lustre even on their dignity. To all the polish and refinement of their Nation, was added the charm of humility, which Religion alone can confer. Of that distinguished body, the learned Bishop of Orleans, Monseigneur Dupanloup, though by no means the first in rank, attracted most attention. In one of the Churches of Rome, during our visit, whilst preaching on the sufferings of the Oriental Christians, he carried our minds back to the time when the eloquence of Chrysostom swayed the people of Constantinople, and so thrilled their hearts, as to cause them to forget the sacredness of the place by breaking into frequent demonstrations of applause. This venerable body gathered round the Chair of Peter with characteristic ardor. The honor of France, they loudly asserted, was pledged "for the protection of the Pope. The arms of France were mainly instrumental in bringing him to his present state of helpless dependence, they should now rally round him to maintain him against his foes." Since the return of those fearless souls to their home, all the other Bishops, who were unable to accompany their more fortunate brothers, have, to the number of thirty-five, signed the Address of June 9th, whilst the same testimony of devotion was given by more than 40,000 of their Priests.

To all of that distinguished body now issuing from the collonade of the Vatican, I shall now say, gratefully and affectionately—farewell!

It is expected on an occasion like the present, that I should not pass over the temporal affairs of the Sovereign Pontiff, and his actual relations to his own subjects. Before proceeding to such observations, I shall make some remarks on the origin of his temporal power. From a very early period we find the Pope exercising temporal dominion in Rome. It was never pretended that such power was given in the Commission to Govern the Kingdom of Christ. It arose from circumstances, and from the exigencies of the times. For the first three hundred years the Successors of St. Peter may be said to have stepped from the Pontifical Chair to the scaffold. So far from exercising any temporal sway, the sword was suspended over their necks. But even then we find the Church possessing considerable wealth bestowed by the charity of the early Christians for the maintenance of the orphans, and the relief of the poor. The deacon St. Lawrence, before his martyrdom, distributes all the wealth of the Church to the poor, and when asked for gold, points to them saying, "behold the treasures of the Church."

In the 4th century, Constantine bestowed the Church and Palace of the Lateran on St. Sylvester, assigning at the same time an adequate income for their maintenance. When the Seat of Empire was transferred from the banks of the Tiber to the shores of the Bosphorus, the Chair of Peter was no longer overshadowed by the imperial throne. From that period the temporal influence of the Pontiffs was largely on the increase. The irruptions of the barbarians forced them to assume a position silently conceded them by the Emperor of Constantinople. Attila, called "Scourge of God," with his five thousand Huns was turned back from the gates of Rome, by the majesty of Leo. Two years afterwards he confronts Genseric with his Vandals and Moors, and saves the lives of his people, though he cannot rescue the City from pillage.

In the Sixth Century, Gregory the Great exercises undoubted temporal jurisdiction. Gibbon, not a partial witness of such a cause, thus speaks of his efforts to restore peace to Italy: "Disappointed in the hopes of a general and lasting treaty, he presumed to save his country without the consent of the Emperor, or the Exarch. The sword of the enemy was suspended over Rome; it was averted by the mild eloquence and seasonable gifts of the Pontiff, who commanded the respect of heretics and barbarians. The merits of Gregory were treated by the Byzantine Court with reproach and insult; but in the attachment of a grateful people, he found the purest reward of a citizen, and the best right of a sovereign." In 755 Pepin *restored* to the Pope Stephen III, twenty cities which his valor wrested from the usurpation of the Lombards. "The Popes," says Hallam, "appear to have possessed some measure of temporal power, even while the City was governed by the Exarchs of Ravenna, in the name of the Eastern Empire. This power became more extensive on her separation from Constantinople."

When the Byzantine Court lost all power in Italy, the government of Rome, and of many of its provinces, reverted naturally to those who had long exercised the rights of government, with the tacit or express consent of the Greek Emperor, and the warm approval of the people.

"The want of laws," adds the Historian of the Decline and Fall, "could only be supplied by the influence of Religion, and their foreign and domestic councils were moderated by the authority of the Bishop. His alms, his sermons, his correspondence with the kings and prelates of the West, his recent services, their gratitude and oath, accustomed the Romans to consider him as the first Magistrate, or Prince of the City. The Christian humility of the Popes," adds the "great Master of Irony," "was not offended by the name of *Dominus*, or Lord: and their face and inscriptions are still apparent on the most ancient coins. Their temporal dominion is now confirmed by the reverence of a thousand years, and *their noblest title is the free choice of a people, whom they had redeemed from slavery.*"

The title then by which the present Pontiff holds his temporal domain, called through reverence the Patrimony of St. Peter, is the most just, and most ancient of all earthly Sovereignties. It sprung not from usurpation, or ambition, nor the lust of power or conquest, but from the wants and necessities of the times, and the free choice of the governed. We shall look in vain elsewhere for so venerable, so enlightened a line of sovereigns. Under their influence, not only was Religion propagated, but the domain of Civilization extended, while learning and the Arts always flourished under their fostering care. Whilst the proudest of modern nations had hardly emerged from barbarism, Rome was the centre of light, and of all civilizing influences to the Nations of the earth. Without the far seeing wisdom of its Rulers, we would to-day have as little of the ruins of Rome, as we have of Troy, or Nineveh, or Babylon. Whoever has visited the ancient Capital, will find proofs of this watchful guardianship in every age, in the monuments to be found in her streets, the ruins preserved and sustained at a vast expense, her fountains, her columns, her gardens, in all that a lavish generosity combined with the most perfect taste, could effect for the embellishment of the well beloved City. Under the patronage of the Popes, the Vatican became the repository of the Arts of Greece and ancient Rome, "and buried learning rose redeemed to a new morn."

And what are the feelings of the present Romans towards the present successor of this ancient line of Rulers, compared with which "the proudest royal houses of Europe are but yesterday." In common with many others I went to Rome impressed with the conviction that very many of his subjects disliked his rule, and longed for a change. This I ascribed not to the imperfection of the Papal Government, well knowing its solicitude for the welfare of its subjects, but to the intrigues of its enemies, who cast longing eyes on its coveted possessions. But the signs of this discontent, here and elsewhere falsely represented as so general, I candidly assert were no where visible. On the contrary, wherever Pio Nono appeared, he was every where received with general, and apparently heartfelt enthusiasm. Much of this attachment is doubtless to be ascribed to the charming character of the Pontiff himself,—"a Pope," to use the expression made to myself by a warm partisan of the new order of things in Italy, "worthy in every respect of the best and purest ages of the Church." And this devotion has been increased by the disappointment of many at the unsatisfactory results of their very success in the Central and Northern Parts of Italy, where the desired change has not been attended with that increase of freedom, and of wealth which was confidently expected. Above all, the experience of Naples is not lost upon the inhabitants of Rome. The Bourbon was compelled to fly, and a stranger rules. His armed soldiery everywhere appear, and at the present time, in this its day of reported freedom, the prisons and dungeons of Naples are more fearfully crowded than in any period of the unhappy history of that enchanting City.

A French nobleman, whose acquaintance I formed in Rome, in the course of conversation one day, thus addressed me: "I am much pleased that I have come to Rome, for many reasons, but for one especially. I really believed that the Romans disliked the Pope as a temporal Ruler, but never have I seen such attachment to a man, as I have every day witnessed towards him; and as far as I can learn from my own observation, and from the information of others, they are contented and happy." And such was the general impression of all who visited Rome during the late Solemnity. It must not be concealed, however, that the Revolutionary party is active and vigilant, and by no means scrupulous in the attainment of its ends. It is not improbable that it may succeed for a time, and that Pius IX, like so many of his predecessors, may be an exile from his venerable See. But he, or his successors will be brought back in triumph to that City, which is maintained only by Religion, and which, without the Popes, would long since have been reduced to a heap of undistinguished ruins.

The world too, is begining to feel the necessity of the temporal independence of the Pope, for the interests of Religion and of society. His ancient patrimony is not large enough for the ends of ambition, or aggression, but it secures him from being the subject of any foreign Power. The Catholic world, now numbering two hundred million souls, can freely communicate with him in his own small principality, without obstruction, or scrutiny. The hand of Providence is clearly traced in its wonderful preservation through so many ages, while so many powerful nations have arisen and disappeared—its very weakness proving to be its strength, and its most powerful support often coming from the arms of the avowed enemies of the Holy See. In no age has this interposition been more strikingly manifested than in our own.

As an instance of the attachment of the Romans to their present amiable Ruler, I need only allude to the ceremony of laying the corner stone of a new barracks, followed by a review of the small, but well drilled army of the Government, on the site of the ancient Pretorian Camp. Probably more than fifty thousand spectators were present on the occasion, which was partly a religious and partly a civil spectacle. Occupying a position near the person of the Pontiff, I enjoyed a favorable opportunity of observing what passed, and of noting the feelings of many present. The few who remained of the Irish Brigade, were ranged round the Prelate, who performed the religious ceremony. This concluded, the army proceeded to pass before the chair of their sovereign. As the various corps of cavalry, infantry and artillery swept past in excellent order, they were loudly applauded. But there was one Brigade of fine material, and surpassing equipments, awaited with the most impatient eagerness. As they approached in gallant style, I noticed they had not only the martial bearing of soldiers, but for the most part, the appearance of gentlemen. As they went by in proud array, the enthusiasm of the multitude knew no bounds. Every voice was loud in acclamation, every hand raised in delight, and a prolonged shout of applause went up from that mighty throng such as was never heard before, even on that spot, before the most popular Emperor of Rome.

On inquiry, I learned that this favorite corps which elicited such universal approval, was the famous Brigade of Pontifical Zouaves, composed for the greater part, of noble volunteers from France and Belgium, and who at Castel Fidardo and Ancona, though overwhelmed by numbers, showed themselves worthy of their noble lineage, and approved themselves true knights, and Christian gentlemen.

But whatever may be the final issue of this struggle between right and injustice,—between patient weakness and remorseless strength,—whether retaining possession of his ancient rights, or despoiled of them by the ruthless hand of power, the Headship of the Church will, in all cases continue the same. The Pope in prison or in exile, whether dwelling a subject in foreign land, or immersed in the Catacombs like many of his predecessors, will disappoint the malice of all who hope for the fall of the Papacy. He would still, in every event, be the successor of St. Peter—still the visible Head of the Church, and his paternal voice coming from prison or exile, would find as prompt an obedience from the heart of every Catholic, as if issuing from his Chair in St. Peter, or his throne in the Vatican.

But we must bid farewell, however unwillingly, to Rome, and to all the visions and reflections it awakens. The time elapsed permits me to trespass on your attention no longer.

What general conclusions, then, are to be drawn from all you have so patiently listened to? They are obvious to the least reflecting mind—the divine power of the Church, living and effectual—its unity and universality. A mere word of invitation proceeds from the Chair of St. Peter, and the entire Catholic world is profoundly moved. From all quarters of the Universe, the representatives of the Catholic City, the Successors of the Apostles, regardless of the fatigues and perils of the way, hasten to the Centre of Unity. Still larger would have been that attendance, if affairs of the deepest moment had not detained many, reluctantly, at home. But from the remote lands they come, and are arranged in holy phalanx around the Chair of St. Peter. Even remote Africa, and Islands set far away in the mighty ocean, and half civilized countries had their Christian representatives in Rome. What power, not from above, could have convened such an assemblage? What principle, other than divine, could thus make its influence felt and acknowledged in the very extremities of the earth?

And that revered body differed among themselves in many things,—in rites, in forms of government, in laws, in language, nay, even in their very dress; but in one important point they were harmonious—all divinely one—in faith—in attachment to the Chair of Peter—the keystone of the arch of the building raised by divine hands, the centre of Religion, of civilization, and of learning to all parts of the Universe. Yes! This grand demonstration in our days, proves the ever living and active power of God's Church.

It is no less convincing of its divine perpetuity. All other Institutions give mournful evidence of their human origin. They spring but to fall, they flourish to decay. However powerful they appear, they are sure of being overtaken by the irresistible stroke of time. It is the doom that awaits all the works of man, however durable they seem, however ardently we long for their immortality. But the Church, the City of God, not built by human hands, is proof wasting touch of decay,—knows not the decrepitude of age, but blooms in unfading youth, and ever operates with eternal vigor.

In our own times she glows with the same divine life as in the days of the Apostles, and burns with the same zeal for the enlightenment of the nations, and for the improvement of mankind. Though passing through many trials, she always rises superior to them all. The bark of Peter is borne triumphant over the waves that buffet her,—the Ark of the New Covenant floats in tranquil majesty over the deluge of waters that threaten to engulf her. She is now what she has ever been, unchanged and unchangeable—the source of light and of true civilization to the world, and animated by a divine life, guided by the Holy Spirit ever dwelling in her, she will continue to discharge her duty on earth, by enlightening the minds of men, moving and guiding their hearts, and sanctifying their souls, until her mission on earth be accomplished—till all that is mortal in man shall put on immortality, and time itself be merged into Eternity.

www.ingramcontent.com/pod-product-compliance
Lightning Source LLC
Chambersburg PA
CBHW021456090426
42739CB00009B/1756

* 9 7 8 3 3 3 7 1 6 8 6 8 1 *